Johnny Bench

Jesse Jarnow

the rosen publishing group's
rosen
central

Published in 2004 by The Rosen Publishing Group, Inc.
29 East 21st Street, New York, NY 10010

First Edition

Library of Congress Cataloging-in-Publication Data

Jarnow, Jesse.
Johnny Bench/by Jesse Jarnow.—1st ed.
    p. cm.—(Baseball Hall of Famers)
Summary: A biography of Cincinnati Reds' catcher,
Johnny Bench, who won ten Gold Glove awards and hit
almost 400 home runs in his sixteen-year career in the
major leagues.
Includes bibliographical references and index.
ISBN 0-8239-3780-1 (library binding)
1. Bench, Johnny, 1947—Juvenile literature. 2. Baseball
players—United States—Biography—Juvenile literature.
[1. Bench, Johnny, 1947—2. Baseball players.]
I. Title. II. Series.
GV865.B35 J37 2003
796.357'092—dc21

                                          2002012129

Manufactured in the United States of America

Contents

In recognition of his great career, an emotional Johnny Bench is presented with his Hall of Fame plaque in Cooperstown, New York, in 1989.

Introduction

Johnny Bench stood in the warm summer sunshine and looked out over the crowd gathered in the parking lot in Cooperstown, New York. Behind him stood the Baseball Hall of Fame. Around him were family, friends, and fellow ballplayers. They were there to honor him as one of the greatest baseball players—and most important catchers—of all time. "It is a great privilege and honor to be with my idols," he said. It was a long way from Binger, Oklahoma, where—growing up—he had watched Mickey Mantle on television and dreamed of playing pro ball.

When Johnny Bench made it to the major leagues in 1967, he redefined how people thought about catchers. Not only was he an amazing catcher, but he was a powerful hitter.

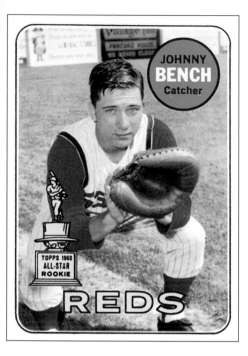

JOHNNY
BENCH
Catcher

TOPPS 1968
ALL-STAR
ROOKIE

REDS

Johnny Bench confidently predicted that he would win the National League Rookie of the Year Award in 1969, and he was right. In a baseball card commemorating this accomplishment, Bench is pictured holding his mitt with two hands. A style popular with the catchers of the day, it was something Johnny never did. Instead, he originated catching with one hand, keeping his throwing hand behind his back to protect it from foul tips.

He won ten Gold Glove awards for his legendary defense, and hit almost 400 home runs in a sixteen-year career—the most any catcher had ever hit!

Johnny stayed with one team, the Cincinnati Reds, for his entire career (a rarity in modern baseball). He was a proud member of what was known as "the Big Red Machine," one of the strongest teams ever to play the game. Shoulder-to-shoulder with other celebrated players (such as Pete Rose, Tony Perez, Lee May, and George Foster), Bench helped the team to several pennants and two World Series wins.

The circumstances of Bench's career were not extraordinary. He did not face discrimination or hardship in becoming a professional baseball player. But there was nothing he wanted to do more. He was an average kid from the middle of Oklahoma who proved that with concerted effort and a deep passion for the game, he could be a great ballplayer.

Always confident, Bench appears calm before taking the field in this June 1982 photo.

Oklahoma, Okay!

J onathan Lee Bench was born on December 7, 1947 in Oklahoma City, Oklahoma, to Ted and Katy Bench. He was the third of four children. His brothers, Teddy and William, were older, and his sister, Marilyn, was nineteen months younger. Johnny's father drove a truck for a local gas company. The family moved around a lot—from Oklahoma City to Lindsay, to Aaron Springs, and finally to Binger. By the time they got to Binger, Johnny had begun playing baseball.

It was a tradition. Ted Bench had been a top-notch baseball player when he was younger. Like Johnny, he was a catcher. When he got back from fighting in World War II, though, he was too old to be considered for the majors. Instead, he played semiprofessional ball in a variety of regional leagues. He even played against future Hall of Famer Satchel Paige. He raised Johnny, Teddy, and William to be ballplayers, and established a Little League team for them to play on called the Binger Bobcats. He made Johnny the catcher.

As in most places in America at the time, baseball was extremely popular in Binger. The kids played so much that they had to cover their bats and balls with electrical tape just to hold them together. They played on sandlots and in empty fields—anywhere where there was room, and some places where there wasn't. Johnny once saw his father hit a ball far into a nearby cornfield. "In my mind, nobody has yet hit a ball further," he wrote in his autobiography, *Catch You Later.*

When they didn't have baseballs to use, the kids would use old milk cans. The cans flew every which way. Johnny later said that trying to hit the cans prepared him to hit breaking balls, curveballs, sliders, and sinkers. It was dangerous, though, and Johnny once cut his finger on a can's metal edge. He still has the scar.

The little town of Binger, Oklahoma, will always be remembered as the place where Johnny Bench grew up. In 1970, Binger had a population of 730 people, offering Johnny few distractions to keep his mind off baseball.

Bench's hero Mickey Mantle warms up with a few pregame swings in Yankee Stadium. Mantle was another ballplayer from Oklahoma. Growing up, Johnny seldom missed one of Mantle's games on television.

Whenever his teachers asked him what he wanted to be when he grew up, Johnny said that he wanted to be a professional baseball player. But the kids in his class laughed at him because he was so short and small. He had big hands and feet, though. "Don't worry," his father told him, "you'll grow into them." Most important, he was a good ballplayer. Despite his size, his older brothers took him along whenever they played.

Johnny was obsessed with baseball. When he wasn't playing, he was watching it on television or thinking about it. He practiced his penmanship for school by pretending to sign autographs. On Saturdays, the family would buy ice cream and watch the game of the week on television. It was then that Johnny first laid eyes on Mickey Mantle.

Though Mantle was with the New York Yankees, he was from Oklahoma. The announcers said he was a player to watch. Johnny did. Mickey Mantle, the switch-hitting outfielder from Johnny's home state, became one of his heroes. Johnny was a Yankees fan. He rooted for them in the 1961 World Series when they beat the Cincinnati Reds, Johnny's future team.

Once, Johnny and his friends drove almost 600 miles to St. Louis, Missouri, to see the Cardinals play against the Los Angeles Dodgers. Two of his friends, Larry and Gary Griffith, had a brother named Derrell who was playing for the Dodgers. Jeff Torberg, their

The Home Run Race

In the 1950s, when Johnny was growing up, Babe Ruth of the New York Yankees held the record for the number of home runs hit in a single season. Many players tried to beat it, but nobody could. Johnny's hero, Mickey Mantle, was one of them. In 1961, Mantle hit up a storm. By the end of the season, he had racked up 54 homers, just six away from Ruth's record. Mantle's teammate, Roger Maris, broke it that same year with 61 home runs. Maris's record held for thirty-seven years when both Mark McGwire and Barry Bonds broke it.

catcher, gave Gary a catcher's mitt. Gary gave it to Johnny. It was Johnny's first catcher's mitt.

While he was in St. Louis, Johnny studied all the pro players' moves. He took notes about whether or not they signed autographs or if they needed a shave. He compared what he saw to what he had seen in *Sports Illustrated*. He saw players smoking in the bullpen, and decided that he never wanted to do that. Likewise, he once saw his parents yell at each other after

Bench lurches over the Phillies' dugout for a foul ball in 1972. Bench's trademark backward batting helmet would soon be adopted by all major league catchers.

they got drunk at a bar. He decided that he would never drink, either. His father stopped drinking after he started going to church.

When he was fifteen, Johnny finally started to grow a lot. He grew eight inches in one year! Suddenly, it wasn't so funny when Johnny said he wanted to be a pro ballplayer. He played in the American Legion league and toured all over Oklahoma with the team, playing games in Anadarko, Oklahoma City, and Fort Cobb. Needless to say,

When Bench was a teenager, his father had him practice throwing 254 feet from a crouch—twice the distance from home plate to second base.

Johnny was better than most of the players in the league. He hit almost .700 during one season. Sometimes Johnny pitched, too. He was just as good! He had prepared for throwing runners out by throwing twice the distance to second base. Since a pitcher only has to throw half that distance, it's no wonder he threw a smoking fastball. He racked up a 75-3 winning record.

Johnny's father watched many of the games. Lots of local folks came out to watch, too. People in Oklahoma loved baseball.

Johnny played so much baseball that he often came home late. Once, he covered himself in dirt and told his mother that he had gotten into a fight. She started to wash his face and realized that he was lying. Johnny knew then that he couldn't lie to his mother. She'd catch him for sure.

Johnny went to a very small school. There were twenty-one people in his class. The people on the basketball team were the same people on the baseball team, so Johnny played basketball, too. In high school, Johnny made honorable mention as an all-American forward.

Nicknames

Baseball players have always had distinctive nicknames. The kinds of names have changed over time. In the 1950s, animal nicknames were very popular. Some of these included Roy "Squirrel" Sievers, Don "The Weasel" Bessent, Harvey "The Kitten" Haddix, Frank "Pig" House, and Duke "The Silver Fox" Snider. Nicknames in the 1960s got even funnier. Some players included Ed "The Creeper" Stroud, Jimmie "The Toy Cannon" Wynn, Mike "Moonman" Shannon, Dick "Dr. Strangeglove" Stuart, Paul "Motormouth" Brown, and "Marvellous" Marv Throneberry.

Johnny was also a good student. He was the valedictorian in junior high school and high school. Being valedictorian means he had the highest grades in his class.

Johnny worked at many part-time jobs. Picking cotton, he earned two cents for every pound that he picked. He also picked peanuts and worked for the Binger Peanut Company. Johnny built up his strength by loading

Mugging for the camera, Bench takes a moment off from spring training to show off his large hands by holding up seven baseballs at once.

100-pound bags of peanuts into trucks. He wore goggles to protect his eyes from the dust.

Johnny also worked a paper route and mowed people's lawns. As a result, he once said, he knew the names of everybody in town. It was a wonder that he had time to play baseball at all!

With some of his earnings, Johnny bought clothing—boots and blue jeans. He listened to his father's advice, too, and put some of it in the bank.

During Johnny's senior year of high school, tragedy struck. On April first—April Fool's Day—Johnny and his team played a game on the Native American reservation in Riverside. On the way back, they were traveling down a hill when their coach suddenly cried out "We're out of brakes!" At first, Johnny thought it was an April Fool's joke and laughed, but quickly realized his coach was serious. At the bottom of the hill, the bus hit a railing and flipped over. It rolled downhill into a fifty-foot ravine.

Johnny knew that if you were ever in trouble in a bus, you should get on the floor. He grabbed his friend David and pinned him to the floorboards. After the bus had flipped three times, it came to a stop. Boys had been thrown everywhere. Some of them had been thrown out of the windows. Johnny was lying with his feet hanging out of the back door. Thankfully, some of the passengers, including Johnny, were unhurt. But two of the boys—Harold Dean Simms and Billy Wiley—were not. They had been killed.

Johnny was deeply affected by the sudden death of his friends. A few years later, two more boys on the team (who were home sick that day), also met premature ends. Both were excellent athletes and good friends. Johnny has said it is because of these accidents that he sometimes has a hard time making close friends.

All the while, Johnny continued to play baseball. He kept getting better.

The Next Catcher for the Cincinnati Reds

Needless to say, professional baseball teams were interested in Johnny. The Chicago Cubs scouted him during a game at Lake Tenkiller. Johnny was tired, though, and had a bad day. The Cubs ended up looking at somebody else. Tony Robello, a scout for the Cincinnati Reds, saw Johnny play and was very impressed. He made Johnny a good offer. On June 21, 1965, Johnny signed with the Cincinnati Reds. He was seventeen years old.

Two days later, Johnny's father took him to the airport in Oklahoma City. Johnny said goodbye and got on an airplane bound for Tampa, Florida. It was his first time on an airplane. He was going to join the Tampa Tarpons, one of the Reds' minor league teams.

He got to Tampa at nine o'clock at night. Somebody from the team picked him up and drove him directly to the stadium. Johnny put on his new uniform and went to the field. Right away, in the seventh inning, he warmed up a pitcher in the bullpen. In the eighth inning, he warmed up a pitcher behind home plate. In the ninth inning, Johnny was put in the game. By the next day, the manager Cactus Jack Cassini had made him the team's starting catcher.

Johnny enjoyed playing for Tampa, but felt it was almost too easy. They didn't play many games, and the competition wasn't very hard. Playing in Florida, the team got rained out a lot. But at the end of the season, when the team had to make up all of the rained out games, they played thirteen doubleheaders in fifteen days. Johnny got worn out and played poorly.

That winter, Johnny stayed in Florida and played in the instructional league. After living by himself in the Tampa Park and Sleep Motel, he moved in with Bob and Mildred Sparks. The Sparks's son, Mike, was the team's batboy. They

The Minor Leagues

Minor league baseball games can often be more exciting than major league games. There are hundreds of minor league baseball teams across the country. They are in small towns, big cities, and everywhere in between. Tickets are cheaper. The stadiums are smaller. Teams often have all kinds of wacky promotions and giveaways to get people out to the parks. Some people say that minor league baseball is purer than major league ball. It's also a chance to see the stars of tomorrow in action.

When the minor leagues were formed in the early twentieth century, they were seen as no less worthy than the majors. With dozens of leagues across the nation, the minors simply became regional alternatives to the majors. Gradually, though, the major league clubs began to buy the teams. They used them as a so-called "farm system" to develop talent.

By the 1960s, a formal hierarchy had developed. After players were drafted, they joined the A-level team. They moved up to the AA (double A) and AAA (triple A) teams before graduating to "The Show." The minors are not just for young players. Local fans have their favorite all-stars who have often played with their hometown minor league teams.

treated Johnny like a son, fixing him breakfast and doing his laundry. Johnny worked hard and began to improve. People noticed. The farm bulletins reported that Johnny was going to be the next catcher for the Reds.

In the spring of 1966, Johnny went to spring training with the major league team. Don Heffner, the Reds' manager, gave Johnny a choice. Johnny could be the backup catcher on the big league team or he could be the starting catcher on a minor league team. Johnny chose the minors because he knew he would get in more playing time. He joined the Peninsula Grays, the Reds' Class A team from Virginia.

At first Johnny didn't do well. He developed a bad temper, which only made things worse. Occasionally, he threw his batting helmet when he played poorly. To remind himself not to break it, he began to wear the helmet backward underneath his catcher's mask. Johnny discovered that wearing his helmet backwards helped protect him from getting hurt by foul balls or bad swings. Today many catchers do the same thing. It was an accidental innovation, but it worked.

Once Johnny had his temper under control, he began to have a great season. In 93 games, Johnny hit 23 home runs. Once, he hit nine home runs in nine days. There was a store that gave free suits away to players when they hit home runs that sailed over the store's advertisement in the outfield. Johnny hit ten homers over the sign and got ten free suits.

He was named Player of the Year. Soon, Johnny was called up to the team's AAA team in Buffalo, New York. During the first inning of the first game, Johnny got hit by a foul ball and broke his thumb. That was the end of his season.

Johnny went back to Binger to visit. In August, he went to Wichita to watch his friend play in an exhibition game. After the game, Johnny began to drive back to Oklahoma City. In the middle of the night, a drunk driver pulled onto the highway going in the wrong direction. He was coming right at Johnny! Johnny tried to swerve out of the way. The other driver clipped Johnny's car, and Johnny's car skidded and hit the barrier. Johnny was hurt in the accident, but it could have been worse. He needed twenty-seven stitches in his forehead, but his seatbelt had saved his life.

After doing basic army training at Fort Knox and Fort Dix, Johnny reported back to the team in Buffalo. The team had a bad year, but Johnny did well. There were many young players like Johnny on the team, but there were also older players who hadn't played so well in the majors. They had been sent back down to the minors. Johnny learned a lot by watching and talking to them.

At the end of August 1967, Johnny was called up to the big leagues! Dave Bristol was the Reds' new manager. Having heard great things about Johnny, Bristol wanted Johnny to play for him.

As soon as Johnny arrived at the Reds' stadium, Crosley Field, he was put into the game. The Reds were playing the Philadelphia

Temperamental manager Dave Bristol *(left)* shakes hands with Bench during 1969 spring training. Bristol was fired later that year.

Phillies. Johnny hit a double and a sacrifice fly. He was on his way. Johnny moved into the Vernon Manor, a residential hotel where some of the other players lived.

Bristol wanted to play Johnny every day. So he did. Johnny was happy to play a lot, but he was also worried about the Rookie of the Year award. Johnny wanted to win the award. If a player has over 90 at-bats in a season, then he is eligible for the award. But if Johnny kept playing, he would have played too many games to qualify. At the very end of the season, when he was about to go over 90 at-bats, Johnny injured his thumb again. He sat out the last few games. In 1968, he would qualify.

Johnny had played in 26 games during his month in the big leagues. He hit only .167 and had just one home run. He wanted to improve, so he went to Puerto Rico to play in a winter league. His manager there, Don Zimmer, pushed Johnny hard. Johnny did very well. He hit over .300 in Puerto Rico, though he didn't get too many home runs. Then, a local store started giving away watches for every home run. Johnny won five in one week.

Catching is probably the toughest position in baseball. Catchers get injured quite easily. Johnny tried to come up with ways to keep himself safe. He continued to wear his batting helmet backward underneath his catcher's mask. To protect his throwing hand, he started to catch in a new way. He had seen catcher Randy Hundley of the Chicago Cubs hold his mitt in front of him. At the same time, he tucked his throwing hand behind his back where it would not be vulnerable to foul balls or anything else.

At the beginning of 1968, Johnny set out to win the Rookie of the Year award. Though the Reds didn't do very well that season, Johnny had a good year. He hit .275 and smashed 15 home runs. Having practiced his defense before every game, he had gotten quite good at scooping wild balls out of the dirt. As a result, Johnny won his first Gold Glove award. He would win nine more of them over the course of his career. More important to Johnny, though, he won the

On November 22, 1968, Johnny Bench was all smiles, and with good reason. He had just been named National League Rookie of the Year, a promising beginning to a career that would ultimately lead him into the Baseball Hall of Fame.

Rookie of the Year award. He was the first catcher to do so.

The Reds finished in fourth place that season with an 83-79 record. They were behind the St. Louis Cardinals, the San Francisco Giants, and the Chicago Cubs. Though most of his teammates weren't very good players, Johnny spent time getting to know them. Many were colorful characters, like George Culver, Tommy Helms,

Wayne "Stick" Granger, "Bullet" Bob Lee, Jim "Titser" Maloney, and Jim Merritt, the "Badger." The team was also accumulating great players like Pete Rose, Tony Perez, and Lee May. Rose was the best leadoff hitter in baseball. He would eventually break Ty Cobb's record for all-time hits.

By 1969, Johnny was hitting cleanup. He had another great year, proving that he wasn't just a one-year wonder. Johnny became a much better catcher, too. He was a smart catcher. He studied the hitters. He called pitches. Johnny also had a great record for throwing base runners out when they tried to steal. Most catchers only caught 25 percent of the runners. Johnny caught 50 percent of them.

Johnny built a reputation for being a hardworking catcher. The reputation was both good and bad. He earned the nickname "the Little General." It meant that he liked to have things his way. Sometimes, pitchers didn't like the way Johnny told them what they should pitch. Many times, though, Johnny was right. People respected him for this.

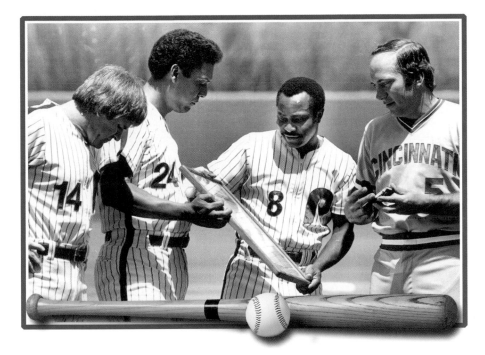

The stars of Cincinnati's Big Red Machine—Pete Rose, Tony Perez, Joe Morgan, and Johnny Bench—gather together during a pregame ceremony.

But the Reds still weren't winning enough games. In 1969, Johnny had a great year, and Pete Rose led the league in hitting. But the Reds finished in third place, behind the Atlanta Braves and the San Francisco Giants. It was also the first year of divisional play. Each league had divided into two divisions: the eastern division and the western division. The Reds were now in the western division. To get to the World Series,

Johnny Bench digs in as Orlando Cepeda of the Atlanta Braves comes barreling in toward home plate. A base runner trying to score a run often collides with the catcher in an attempt to get him to drop the ball.

the eastern division champions had to play the western division champions in the playoffs.

Dave Bristol was a tough manager. Johnny and Bristol didn't get along all the time. Bristol sometimes threw temper tantrums if the team did badly. He hurled things around the clubhouse. Sometimes, it seemed like he was mad at Johnny for getting so much attention. In truth, he just wanted other players on the team to be recognized as much as Johnny. At the end of the season he was fired, and was replaced by George Lee "Sparky" Anderson.

Building the Big Red Machine

S parky Anderson hadn't been a very good baseball player. But he was an excellent manager. Before he managed the Reds, he managed minor league teams in Rock Hill, South Carolina; St. Petersburg, Florida; and Asheville, North Carolina. He had been a used-car salesman, too. Though he was only thirty-five years old, he looked much older. He had white hair. He got along with the team much better than Dave Bristol had. The players respected Sparky because, instead of yelling, he talked calmly to them.

The Reds had earned the nickname "the Big Red Machine." Everybody was playing the best baseball of his life. During the first half of the season, the Reds went 70-30. They were unstoppable. A pitcher named Wayne Simpson won 12 games in the first half of the season.

George Lee "Sparky" Anderson replaced Dave Bristol as manager of the Reds in 1969. His upbeat personality ensured that he was well-liked by his players.

The All-Star game was held in Cincinnati that year. Many of Johnny's friends from Oklahoma came to see him play. Johnny was hitting lots of home runs. In the middle of the season, the team moved to Riverfront Stadium, which had AstroTurf instead of natural grass.

Everybody loved the Reds. Newspaper and magazine writers interviewed them. Sparky charmed the press with his own brand of humor. Sparky named Pete Rose as the team's captain. Though Johnny was disappointed that he wasn't named captain himself, he understood. Pete was from Cincinnati. He was an extremely hard-working player and a good inspiration to other team members. He concentrated on baseball completely and totally.

Another player, Tony Perez, gave the team a sense of humor. Perez was the team's first baseman. His humor helped bond the players together. "He grew up in Camagüey, Cuba, just about as far away in style from Binger, Oklahoma, as you can get," Johnny wrote in his autobiography. "But nobody had more of an

51,050 fans turn up to welcome the Reds at the brand-new Riverfront Stadium on June 30, 1970. It would take some time for the Reds to adjust to playing on the stadium's AstroTurf.

influence on me." Perez ribbed his teammates gently. The baseball season is long. High spirits are important. In his own way, Perez was as important as Rose to the Big Red Machine.

The Reds weren't as successful in the second half of the season. They won only 32 games and lost 30. Many players, including Wayne Simpson, were injured. Johnny managed

AstroTurf

AstroTurf was developed in the early 1960s for use at the Houston AstroDome. A fake grass, it was later used in the Cincinnati Reds' Riverfront Stadium. Many teams in baseball, football, and other sports choose AstroTurf because it is easier to maintain than natural grass. They do not have to cut or water it. If some of it accidentally gets ripped up, they do not have to replant it; they simply have to lay more down.

AstroTurf changed the way baseball was played. Balls bounce higher on AstroTurf than they do off real grass playing fields. Fielders have to use different strategies to catch bouncing balls. But AstroTurf provided reliability. Balls couldn't bounce unpredictably off a rock hidden in the grass. Many people do not like AstroTurf. They think that because it is synthetic, it is impure.

to stay healthy, finishing with an amazing year. He topped the entire major leagues with 45 home runs and 148 runs batted in. The Reds had done well enough in the first half of the season to win their division. In fact, they had done so well that they won it by over 14 games!

To get to the World Series, the Reds had to play the Pittsburgh Pirates in the second National League playoffs. The Pirates played at Three Rivers Stadium. As the Reds had done with Riverfront Stadium, the Pirates had moved into Three Rivers Stadium in the middle of the season. And, also like Riverfront Stadium, the field was covered with AstroTurf instead of real grass. The two fields were very much alike. Both teams were still adjusting to their new homes. It seemed as if there was no home field advantage for either team.

The Reds didn't hit very well during the playoffs. In fact, they relied mostly on their pitching. This surprised even them. Even so, the Reds managed to win the first two games fairly easily. For the third game, the teams went back to Cincinnati. Finally, Johnny started to hit. He connected for a home run in the first inning that put the team ahead 2–1. The Pirates tied it up, though. In the eighth inning, the Reds pulled out one more run, and

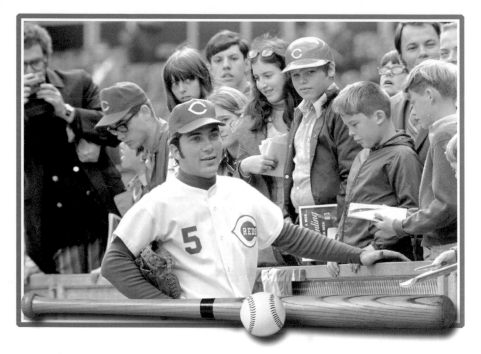

Bench signs autographs for his young fans on the first day of the 1970 World Series against the Baltimore Orioles.

they held on in the ninth. The league championship was theirs!

The Reds went up against the Baltimore Orioles in the World Series. The Orioles had lost the World Series in 1969 to the New York Mets. They had something to prove. The Orioles also had Brooks Robinson, an excellent third baseman and hitter. In the first game, Robinson hit a home run to win the game for the Orioles.

He also stopped many sharply hit balls before they could make their way into the outfield.

Johnny hit a home run in the second game, but the Reds still lost 6–5. The teams went to Baltimore for the third game. Robinson kept playing well. He snagged one of Johnny's line drives. The Reds lost again, 9–3.

In the fourth game, the Reds came back. Though Robinson had four hits, including one home run, the Reds managed to pull out a 6–5 victory. After the game, Johnny even stopped a thief from stealing a woman's purse.

The Reds got off to a good start in game five. They were up 3–0. Unfortunately, the Orioles came back just as quickly. Robinson stopped another one of Johnny's line drives. The Orioles won the game 9–3, and Johnny Bench's first World Series was over.

After the season, Johnny was given many awards for his fine performance. He won his first National League MVP award. He also won the Major League Player of the Year award, the CBS Player of the Year award, and many others.

Johnny won many endorsements, too. He began to do commercials for a variety of products. Johnny appeared on television talk shows, including those hosted by Merv Griffin, Mike Douglas, and Dinah Shore. He enjoyed singing on TV. Earlier in the year, *Life* magazine had called him "Johnny Cash in shin guards" after the famous folk-country star. Johnny also kept himself busy making speaking appearances at banquets.

Comedian Bob Hope invited Johnny to participate in his celebrity golf tournament. Johnny drove a Rolls-Royce and met singer Frank Sinatra and Vice President Spiro Agnew. Johnny's partner in the golf tournament was legendary golfer Arnold Palmer.

Johnny even hosted his own television show called *The MVP Show!*, which ran for three years. Johnny interviewed other celebrities like Willie Mays, Glen Campbell, and—his new friend—Bob Hope. Johnny had fun acting. He later guest starred in an episode of *Mission: Impossible.*

When Bob Hope invited Johnny to join him on a USO tour in Vietnam, Johnny was nervous about going. After all, many of the soldiers in the Army were his age, yet Johnny wasn't fighting. Many ballplayers, including Johnny, had Army reserve status, which meant that they were only on emergency call. Likewise, Johnny knew many boys from Oklahoma who were fighting in the war, some of whom were killed.

Hope's tour was a whirlwind. They ran on a rigorous schedule. The tour stopped in Danang, Long Binh, and Hue in Vietnam, as well as Alaska, Korea, Thailand, and Saudi Arabia, and many soldiers thanked Johnny for taking the time to visit them.

Johnny had fun on the USO tour. Once, when they were performing on a ship, Johnny dressed up like a crewmember and walked onstage. Bob Hope was totally surprised. After that, Johnny and Bob Hope became better friends.

Unfortunately, on the field, 1971 was not the year Johnny Bench and the Reds wanted it to be. After an incredible season in 1970, everybody expected big things. Johnny started off the year very well, hitting nine home runs in the first three

The Cleanup Spot

The cleanup hitter is an important part of many managers' strategies. The first three hitters in the batting order are expected to get on base through singles, doubles, and occasionally triples. They are usually fast runners who can steal bases. The fourth batter—the cleanup hitter—is expected to "clean up" by clearing the bases. He can drive the runners home either by hitting a home run or knocking a deep sacrifice fly into the outfield.

In the years Johnny played, many managers were putting catchers in the eighth position, just above the pitcher (who almost always bat ninth because they are traditionally poor hitters). Johnny wanted very badly to hit cleanup, like his hero Mickey Mantle, but manager Dave Bristol batted him eighth. Early in his career he told one of his coaches that he wanted to be higher in the lineup. The coach passed it along to the manager. Soon, Johnny moved up in the lineup.

weeks. The Reds, however, weren't playing good baseball. People formed bad habits and played poorly. Johnny was one of them. He hit only half the amount of home runs he had in the previous year. His batting average dropped to .238. He hit less than half the RBIs he had in 1970.

There were many reasons why Johnny wasn't doing well. While he hadn't sustained any serious injuries, he was always recovering from small hurts. In addition, Johnny was swinging at bad pitches and holding back on good ones. He tried to improve by using new helmets, batting stances, bats, and grips. He watched videos of his old performances. He studied photographs. At the same time, he was catching and calling nearly every game. Johnny often shared pitchers' frustrations when they lost.

It seemed that the Big Red Machine had disappeared nearly as soon as it had arrived. Crowds in Riverfront Stadium now booed Johnny when he stepped to the plate. Newspaper articles said that Johnny was washed up. Sparky was personally offended that Johnny was being booed. The manager often spoke out for Johnny, defending the star catcher. He couldn't understand why fans would treat Johnny so rudely.

The Reds Reach the Playoffs

At the end of the 1971 season, Johnny and Pete Rose had a fight. The next year, they knew they had to get along to enable the team to win. They needed to help get the Big Red Machine working again. When the Reds started winning, Johnny and Pete forgot about their differences. The team had a great year. It was almost as if 1971 had never happened.

Johnny's friend Lee May was traded to the Houston Astros. In return, the Reds got Joe Morgan, one of the greatest second basemen of all time. He was a great hitter, a very good fielder, and a fast base runner. He hit in the second position, following Pete. Morgan was followed by Bobby Tolan. After Tolan, it was Johnny who hit in the cleanup spot. Johnny's year was almost as good as 1970. In the last week of the season, he had a big streak during which he hit seven home runs in seven days. He finished the season with 40 home runs and 125 RBIs.

The Big Red Machine easily won its division title. Once again, the Reds faced the Pittsburgh Pirates for the league championship. Though the Reds had beaten the Pirates before, even when the Pirates had future Hall of Famers Roberto Clemente and Willie Stargell playing for them, the Pirates were still a very strong team. Their pitching wasn't great, but neither was the Reds'. Remembering the 1970 World Series, the Reds were very nervous going into the playoffs.

The playoffs began in Pittsburgh. In the first inning of the first game, the Reds' Joe Morgan hit a home run. Don Gullett pitched for the Reds. He had a good fastball, but the Pirates hit him hard that day. The Reds lost the game 5–1.

The Reds came back in the second game. In the first inning, they scored four quick runs. Johnny drove in two of them with a double. Joe Morgan hit a home run. The Reds won the game

Soon to trade in his Astros uniform for the white and red of Cincinnati, Astros second baseman Joe Morgan became a valued addition to the Big Red Machine in 1971.

5–3. It was time to go back to Cincinnati for the next games.

Game three was tough for both teams. Nobody could score. Clay Carroll pitched for the Reds. He was a tough pitcher, but the Pirates got a break. In the eighth inning, the score was tied, 2–2. With one out, the Pirates loaded the bases. The Reds wanted to get Manny Sanguillen to ground into a double play. He grounded the ball, but it was too slow. The Reds could only get one man out. Al Oliver scored. The Reds could not score in the ninth inning. They lost the game 3–2. Now, they had to win two games in a row to get to the World Series.

Ross Grimsley pitched very well for the Reds in the fourth game. The Pirates couldn't score at all. The Reds could, though. They scored seven runs very easily. Grimsley only gave up two hits in the entire game. One of them was a home run by Roberto Clemente. The Reds won 7–1.

It was down to the fifth game. Don Gullett pitched again for the Reds. Again, he performed poorly and Sparky quickly replaced him. It was a close game. By the bottom of the ninth inning, the Pirates were winning 3–2. Johnny led off the inning. The crowd was going crazy. As he got to home plate, somebody called out to him. Johnny turned around to see his mother in the crowd. "Hit a home run," she said and smiled at him. Johnny laughed and went to bat.

Johnny fouled off the first pitch. Dave Giusti got another strike on Johnny. The count went to one ball and two strikes. Giusti threw a palm ball. Johnny swung and connected. The ball rose and rose over Roberto Clemente's head and went far over the right field wall. Johnny hit a home run! His teammates rushed out to hug him.

The stadium erupted with cheers. The score was now tied. Johnny's teammates got on base. George Foster got to third. Hal McCrae was up. The new pitcher threw a wild pitch, and George Foster scored. The Reds won the playoffs!

Now it was time to face the Oakland A's in the World Series. The A's were a tough team. The pressure was on. To keep the Reds calm and connected, Sparky had the team members eat dinner together.

In the first game, the Reds didn't do well. In fact, the A's catcher, Gene Tenace, hit two home runs. Johnny was mad at himself because he couldn't prevent the A's catcher from winning the game for them. But Johnny had made plenty of good plays.

The A's got only one stolen base in the entire World Series that year. The Reds lost the second game, too. Dennis Menke hit a ball that looked like it was going to be a home run. Joe Rudi, the left fielder, jumped and caught it as it went over the wall. The Reds lost 2–1. Then they flew to California to play Oakland on the A's own turf.

The Reds won game three, but only barely. Tony Perez slipped and fell while he was rounding third base. Johnny struck out with two players on base in the eighth inning.

The Reds played well in the fourth game. But in the ninth inning, the A's staged a comeback and won the game 3–2.

Batting in the cleanup position, Bench swings for the fences in front of a hostile Milwaukee crowd. Bench was one of the first catchers who was also a powerful hitter.

Game 5, back in Cincinnati, was a close one. The Reds got an early lead as Pete led off the game with a home run. Gene Tenace kept hitting home runs, though. The A's came back and got the score to 4–2.

In the top of the ninth, the A's got "Blue Moon" Odom to third. Bert Campaneris popped a foul ball. Joe Morgan grabbed it. Odom tagged up and started to run home. Morgan lost his balance, but threw the ball right to Johnny. It was a perfect throw, and Johnny got Odom out at home plate. In the bottom of the ninth, Pete won the game for the Reds with an RBI single.

The Reds did well in Game 6, too. Johnny hit a home run. The team played like they had during the regular season. They beat the A's 8–1.

The A's played great defense in the seventh game. Pete hit well, but the A's caught everything. The team loaded the bases. Hal McCrae hit a ball over the wall, but Angel Mangual jumped and caught it! The Reds tagged up and scored a run, but it still hurt. The Reds lost the game 3–2, and their season was over.

While the Reds were in the playoffs and the World Series, Johnny had been hiding something from his teammates. During a routine physical examination in September, the Reds' team doctor discovered that Johnny had a spot on his lung. Nobody knew what it was. Johnny tested negative for both tuberculosis and histoplasmosis, a fungal lung infection. Johnny had never been a smoker, so he didn't think it could be lung cancer. Nobody could be sure, though. In October, Johnny checked into Holmes Hospital in Cincinnati so doctors could figure it out.

First, the doctors performed a bronchoscopy by inserting a very small camera into his lungs. But the doctors couldn't see anything, so they had to perform lung surgery. On December 7, Johnny's friends threw a party for his twenty-fifth birthday.

Two days later, Johnny had surgery. Dr. Luis Gonzalez removed the spot. The doctor sent it to the lab for analysis. It turned out to be a harmless fungus. It had been a huge

Changes in Baseball

The game of baseball has changed a great deal over the years. It will continue to do so as long as people keep playing it. Some of the changes were subtle. Some of the changes were accidental.

Teams Move

In the 1950s, the number of people going to see baseball games dropped off significantly. Some people blamed this on television. They said that because people could watch games on TV, they would no longer go out to the ballpark. A headline in *Baseball Magazine* in 1952 read "TV Must Go . . . Or Baseball Will!"

In 1953, one of Boston's, teams, the Braves, moved to Milwaukee, Wisconsin. In 1966, they moved again, this time to Atlanta, Georgia.

Some cities had too many teams. New York City alone had three teams—the New York Yankees, the New York Giants, and the Brooklyn Dodgers. There were too many games, with not enough people to watch them. In 1958, the Brooklyn Dodgers moved to Los Angeles. The same year, the New York Giants moved to San Francisco.

Cities were developing rapidly, too. Many people were moving to California in the 1940s and 1950s, making it a growing market for baseball, and leading to the creation of new teams.

Rules Change

Many people thought baseball games were too long. To counteract this, the rules were changed to let a manager visit the pitcher on the mound only once an inning. This allowed games to move more quickly.

In the 1960s, the size of the strike zone was also changed. It had previously been measured from the batter's armpits to the top of his knees. The new rules expanded it from the top of the batter's shoulders to the bottom of his knees. This gave pitchers more chance to pitch strikes. It also made it tougher for hitters. Some people say that the change worked too well. Batters struck out more and hit fewer home runs.

Uniforms Change

In the 1960s, teams began using humorous logos. The Chicago Cubs began to use a bear cub. The Baltimore Orioles changed to a smiling bird.

The Cleveland Indians wore a grinning Native American. The Atlanta Braves used an American Indian, too. Recently, these two logos became controversial, as they offended many Native American groups, who felt that the images portrayed them as cartoonlike stereotypes.

Sleeve length of uniforms changed, too. Many uniforms originally had long sleeves. Over time, the sleeves got shorter and shorter. By the 1960s, some teams didn't have sleeves at all! The Cincinnati Reds, the Pittsburgh Pirates, and the Cleveland Indians instead began to wear button-up tunics with T-shirts underneath.

scare. Johnny recovered from the surgery quickly, and was in Florida playing golf in no time.

By the time Johnny got to spring training in 1973, he was ready to play again. He didn't do as well as the year before, but his performance was respectable. He hit 25 home runs and got 104 RBIs. Pete had an even better year. He had a .338 batting average with 230 hits. A pitcher named Jack Billingham won 19 games. Sparky got to manage the American League All-Star team. The Big Red Machine beat out the Los Angeles Dodgers to win the western division once again.

Instead of the Pirates, the Reds faced the New York Mets in the playoffs. The Mets had staged an amazing comeback that year. In the middle of the summer, they were in last place. They won most of the games in the second half of the season. By the time they got to the play-offs, they were on a roll.

The playoffs started in Cincinnati. The first game was close. By the bottom of the ninth inning, the Mets were winning 1–0. Pete hit a home run over the right center field wall to tie the game. Then it was Johnny's turn. He faced Tom Seaver, who had won the Rookie of the Year award the year before Johnny. When Johnny smashed one in the air down the left field line, he couldn't tell if it would stay fair. Finally, it went over the wall into fair territory. Johnny had hit another ninth-inning home run! The Reds won!

Pete Rose

Pete Rose was one of the greatest baseball players of all time. He played with the Cincinnati Reds from 1963 until 1978. From 1979 until 1983 he played for the Philadelphia Phillies. In 1984 he played for the Montreal Expos. By the end of the season, he had rejoined the Reds, becoming one of baseball's few player-managers. This meant that he was both the team's manager and their regular first baseman.

In 1985, he beat Ty Cobb's all-time record for career hits. By the time he retired in 1986, he had racked up 4,256 hits—more than any other player in history. His career batting average was .303! After he retired as a player, Pete continued to serve as manager for another two years.

In 1988, Pete was accused of gambling. He admitted that he had illegally gambled on some sports, including basketball and football. He was accused of betting on his own team, the Reds. While evidence has shown that he probably did bet on the Reds, it indicates that Pete never bet against them.

Through 1989, when hearings were held about the gambling, it became obvious that Pete had a serious gambling problem. Eventually, baseball commissioner Bart Giamatti placed Pete on what

Under investigation by the commissioner of baseball because of his gambling problem, Pete Rose rubs his eyes wearily during a 1989 game.

was called the "permanently ineligible" list. A year later, the Baseball Hall of Fame ruled that anybody on the "permanently ineligible" list was now ineligible to be elected into the Baseball Hall of Fame. Many people have protested. They say that Pete was one of the greatest baseball players of all time, and he deserves to be a Hall of Famer.

"How that man loves the game of baseball," Johnny wrote of Pete in his autobiography. "And not too many people play it better than he does." Later, Johnny wrote that he was "convinced that nothing could interfere with Pete once he walk[ed] out of the dugout. Certainly not anything like a business setback."

Ignoring the insults of the New York City crowd, Pete Rose triumphantly rounds the bases after a 12th inning home run in game 4 of the 1973 National League playoffs.

The second game was close for a while, too. But the Mets pulled it out in their half of the ninth inning, winning the game 5–0.

The teams went to New York for the third game. The Mets got a quick lead when Rusty Staub hit two home runs in the first two innings. The Reds were playing badly.

In the fifth inning, as Johnny was getting ready to go out to the field, he heard a cheer.

He looked up. He saw that Pete was fighting with Bud Harrelson of the Mets. The benches emptied. The players tangled. Johnny found Pete and pulled him out of it. When order was finally restored, the Mets' fans threw things at Pete. Batteries, garbage, metal nuts, and even a whiskey bottle got tossed onto left field. The Reds lost the game 9–2.

The fourth game went into extra innings. In the eleventh inning, The Reds' Danny Driessen smacked one deep into the outfield. Rusty Staub dove to the wall and caught it. In the twelfth inning, Pete hit a home run. Pete smiled while the crowd booed at him. The Reds won the game!

In the fifth game, the Reds weren't so lucky. The Mets won 9–2. But it wasn't over yet. As soon as the game ended, fans started to jump over the walls. They were chasing Pete. Johnny and the rest of the team guarded Pete as he escaped into the clubhouse.

The Reds and the World Series

After Johnny's operation, he became the head of the athletes' division of the American Cancer Society. He spoke out against smoking cigarettes. He devoted a lot of time to the job and took it very seriously. Johnny talked to Dr. Gonzalez, the man who had performed the surgery on him, and learned about human lungs. He observed the operations of other people as well. Every year in Dayton, Ohio, he helped host the Hike for the Handicapped.

Shortly after the 1973 season, Johnny was in Dayton signing autographs at a department store. Sue Lilly, who worked at the store, introduced him to a boy named Phillip Buckingham. Phillip was four years old and

Bench calmly waits to tag out the Pittsburgh Pirates' left fielder Willie Stargell as he slides into home.

had cancer. An energetic boy with bright eyes, he ran around and smiled a lot. Johnny took an immediate liking to him.

That Christmas, Johnny and Sue threw a party for Phillip. They bought him lots of presents. When they learned that Phillip and his family had to take a bus back and forth to the hospital, they bought Phillip's family a car. Johnny and Sue gave him a pony. The fire department drove him around in their trucks.

Johnny Bench kisses bride Vickie Chesser on the day of their wedding.

Johnny dedicated his first home run of the 1974 season to Phillip, which made Phillip very happy. Despite this, he kept getting sicker. Johnny kept in touch with him.

After the 1974 season (when the Reds finished second place to the Los Angeles Dodgers), Johnny met a woman named Vickie Chesser. She was a model from South Carolina. They instantly fell in love. Johnny had dated a lot of girls and knew that she was special. He was ready to be married. In January 1975, Johnny proposed to Vickie. She said "yes." They set their wedding date for February 21.

Johnny and Vickie wanted to have a big wedding. They invited over 900 guests, including President Gerald Ford! They had a five-foot-high wedding cake, too.

Johnny wanted Phillip to come to the wedding, but Phillip was too sick. Johnny wanted to have a piece of the wedding cake sent to Phillip, but it was too late. Phillip died the morning of February 22. Johnny worked even harder for the American Cancer Society after that. He appeared in television advertisements and attended many benefits.

The 1975 season started on a sad note, as well. Jim McGlothin, a pitcher for the Reds, was also diagnosed with cancer. He wasn't doing very well and had stopped playing ball. Johnny and Pete arranged a benefit for him.

Early in the season, Gary Matthews of the San Francisco Giants collided with Johnny at home plate and injured Johnny's shoulder.

The Green Monster

Charles Henry Taylor built Fenway Park for the Boston Red Sox in 1912. In front of the wall in left field there was a steep ten-foot hill. Fans were allowed to sit on the hill and watch the game from the playing field! A giant wall was constructed behind the hill to keep fans from sneaking into the ballpark without paying. The hill became known as "Duffy's Cliff." It was named for outfielder Duffy Lewis, who was famous for catching balls hit to the ledge. After a few small fires, the stadium was renovated several times. Tom Yawkey, the Red Sox' new owner, was responsible for a lot of the work. In 1933, he had Duffy's Cliff demolished. He started selling advertising on the left field wall. In 1947, the advertisements were covered with green paint. The wall became known as the Green Monster. Because it was so close to home plate (compared to most left field walls), batters loved driving big home runs over it. "[It's] supposed to look like it is standing just in back of the shortstop," Johnny once said. Johnny and the Big Red Machine had their chance in 1975.

Though Johnny kept playing, it hurt him for the rest of the season. Because of the injury, he didn't play very well. He tried all kinds of things to help himself feel better—ice, medication, hot pads. None of them worked.

Johnny didn't have a very good season. But the Reds had a great team. By early September, they had clinched their division, a record for the earliest clinching ever. Not only that, but it was the most games that any team had won in almost seventy years! Johnny also stole 11 bases in 11 tries that season, a rare feat since catchers generally aren't good baserunners, a result of the strain catching puts on their knees. Then the Reds were off to the playoffs, where they would face the Pirates once again.

The Reds breezed through the first two playoff games, winning them 8–3 and 6–1, respectively. But they had more trouble in the third game. John Candeleria was pitching for the Pirates. He struck out 14 batters. In the eighth inning, Pete hit a home run. After that, the Reds had no problem. They won the game 5–3. Johnny, however, had a terrible series. He only got one hit the entire time. It was time to face the Boston Red Red Sox in the World Series.

By the time the Reds got to Boston the weather was nasty and rainy. Johnny came down with a cold. Since the Reds were a National League team, they had never played in Boston. Johnny had never seen the city so he went sightseeing with his friends. The weather was bad, though, and it made Johnny's cold worse. By game time, he had lost his voice.

In the first game, the Red Sox pitched Luis Tiant, a pitcher with an unusual windup. The Reds had trouble hitting against him and lost the game 6–0. The weather was even worse during the second game. The Reds were down 2–1 when a rain delay was called in the seventh inning. Johnny sat in the dugout, wrapped in towels, trying to keep warm. The game continued. Johnny went up in the ninth and smacked a double. But neither Tony Perez nor George Foster were able to get Johnny home. When Dave

After having gone 0 for 15 in the 1975 World Series, Tony Perez sends this ball out of the park in the fourth inning of Game 5.

Concepcion hit a single, Johnny finally charged home. The Reds tied the game. Ken Griffey hit a double and put the Reds in the lead for good, 3–2.

Back in Cincinnati, Johnny started to feel better. The weather was nicer and the Reds were playing in Riverfront Stadium again. The Reds got off to a 5–0 lead, but the Red Sox tied it up. In the tenth inning, the Reds' Eddie Armbrister made a sacrifice bunt. The Red Sox forgot to tag him and the Reds had runners on first and third. Joe Morgan singled Cesar Geronimo home and the Reds won the game 6–5.

The fourth game was tough. The Red Sox pitched Luis Tiant again. Though Johnny got a double and drove in a run, the Reds didn't play well. The Red Sox' Fred Lynn caught one of Ken Griffey's hits to the wall. The Reds lost the game 5–4, tying the World Series 2–2. The Reds made up for it in the fifth game. Johnny got a hit and scored when Tony Perez homered.

The sixth game was in Boston. The Reds began by jumping to a 6–3 lead. In the eighth inning, the Red Sox' Bernie Carbo hit a home run and tied the game 6–6. The Red Sox loaded the bases in the ninth, but the Reds managed to escape. George Foster threw a runner out at home. Then, in the eleventh inning, Joe Morgan hit a ball over the wall. But Dwight Evans reached out and grabbed it. Foiled again! In the bottom of the eleventh, Carlton Fisk, the Red Sox catcher, hit a homer and won the game for the Sox.

Although Johnny was extremely sick with the flu before the seventh game, he played anyway. Whether or not the Reds won he would get to rest the next day! The Red Sox got off to a quick 3–0 start. The Reds played catch-up, though. Tony Perez hit a two-run homer, then Pete drove in another run. In the ninth inning, Joe Morgan drove in Ken Griffey and the Reds were ahead! They held the Red Sox in the ninth, and Johnny won his first World Series!

Though the triumph was sweet, Johnny had a bad off-season. By the end of 1975, he was separated from his wife Vickie, soon to be divorced. After that, the press jumped on him for everything under the sun. Likewise, Johnny's injuries didn't fully heal, and he went into 1976 playing only so-so ball. He hit .238 for the year and spent time on the bench. Thankfully, as a team the Reds still played extremely well and easily won their division.

Near the end of the season, Johnny discovered that his salt intake was low. When he increased it, he began to play better baseball.

Teammates Cesar Geronimo and George Foster congratulate Bench after he hits a home run in Game 4 of the 1976 series. Yankees catcher Thurman Munson, whose career was cut short by a plane crash three years later, looks on.

Toys and Books

Johnny got involved in many outside business ventures, most involving baseball. He endorsed many products. One popular item was the Johnny Bench Batter-Up, a pitching machine that helped young batters work on their swings. Batters could adjust the

Johnny Bench participates in a peanut tossing contest at Mickey Mantle's restaurant in New York City.

contraption for speed as well as for pitches. It tossed fastballs, slow balls, sliders, and knuckleballs.

He also appeared in instructional material, such as calendars, videos, and posters. Louisville Slugger bats appeared with Johnny's name on them.

He co-authored several books about baseball, including *The Complete Idiot's Guide To Baseball* (co-written with Larry Burke); *Major League's Best Shots*; *From Behind The Plate*; *Catching and Power Hitting*; and —his autobiography—*Catch You Later* (co-written with William Brashler).

Johnny got his rhythm back, and some of his injuries began to feel better. He felt stronger. The Reds moved on to the playoffs against the Philadelphia Phillies.

The Reds won the first game easily, 6–3. Although Johnny didn't get any hits, he felt good. The Phillies got off to a quick lead in Game 2. In the fifth inning, the Reds loaded the bases. Tony Perez nailed a ball down the right field line, driving two men in. The Reds won the game 6–2.

The third game was back in Cincinnati. In the ninth inning, the Phillies led 6–4. George Foster led off against Ron Reed. On a 1–2 count, he hit one out of the park. The score was 6–5. Johnny was up next. A good pitch came in and Johnny slammed a home run. The crowd erupted. It must have felt good to contribute again. Johnny tied the score, 6–6. After a single by Dave Concepcion, Ken Griffey drove him home.

The Reds won the game and were off to the World Series. This time, they faced the New York Yankees. Johnny was nervous about playing the Yankees. He had been a Yankees

Members of the Big Red Machine celebrate their 1975 World Series victory over the Boston Red Sox.

fan when he was a kid. He had never played in Yankee Stadium before.

The series began in Cincinnati. Joe Morgan hit a homer to lead off the first inning. Johnny got a triple and drove in a run. The Reds won the game 5–1. The team got off to 3–0 lead in the second game thanks to a double by Johnny. The Yankees caught up, but the Reds won the game in the ninth inning with a single by Tony Perez.

The third game was at Yankee Stadium. Johnny hit a line drive back at pitcher Grant Jackson, who made an amazing catch behind his back. The Reds did well again, winning the game 6–2.

By the ninth inning of Game 4, the score was 3–2 in the Reds' favor. Johnny wanted their lead to be bigger. He hit a three-run homer in Yankee Stadium and put the game over the top. The Reds held the Yankees in the ninth and won their second World Series in a row! Remembering what happened in New York in 1973 when they played the Mets, the Reds left the field quickly.

Johnny Retires

A fter the 1976 season, the Reds had a tough decision to make. Danny Dreissen was coming up fast as a first baseman. To play him, they had to trade Johnny's old friend Tony Perez. This was the end of the Big Red Machine.

The Reds went 88-74 in 1977, and finished in second place. Johnny had a great year, though. He hit .275 and had 31 home runs. He also had 109 runs batted in. At the end of the season, Johnny got a new contract.

In 1978, the team played to another second-place finish. Pete had a 44-game hitting streak in the middle of the season. Johnny sat out some games with injuries. He was getting older.

When the year ended, there was another sign that the Big Red Machine was shutting down. Sparky Anderson was replaced as team manager by John McNamara.

After the season, Johnny got his first taste of sportscasting. During the World Series, he appeared with Al Michaels and former pitcher Don Drysdale to provide game commentary. Johnny put a picture of the three of them in his autobiography. Underneath the picture he wrote, "You may have watched and listened to these three guys during the 1978 World Series. The one on the left would rather have been playing, as he probably said quite a few times."

The next year, in 1979, the team won their division, although they lost in the playoffs to the Los Angeles Dodgers. The team slipped again in 1980, finishing in third place. In 1981, the season was shortened by a players' strike. Even though the Reds had the best record in baseball (66-42), they still did not make the playoffs. Johnny sustained injuries that forced him to switch from catcher to first base. For the rest of his career, he

Basking in the cheers and applause of the crowd, Bench is driven around the infield of Riverfront Stadium during Johnny Bench Night on September 17, 1983.

played mostly first base, catching only occasionally. Sometimes he played third base or outfield.

Catcher is the most dangerous and difficult position in baseball because of the constant action. The squatting stance is so stressful that catchers' knees often wear out. Johnny was frequently in some degree of pain while playing.

In 1975 he had major shoulder surgery. Throughout 1976, he had muscle spasms. In

1978, Johnny injured his back sliding into home plate. By 1981, the injuries had caught up with him. After the 1983 season, Johnny retired.

Johnny had owned businesses since early in his career. In 1971, Johnny, Pete, and a man named Hy Ullner opened a car dealership in Dayton. They also opened a bowling alley. Neither of them did very well. Johnny didn't have much time to pay attention to them. He was too busy playing baseball. But once he was retired, he got more involved in business ventures.

Johnny also opened two restaurants. They were called Johnny Bench's Home Stretch (in Kentucky) and Johnny Bench's Home Plate (in Cincinnati). The Home Stretch was decorated in a horse racing theme. Waiters dressed up like jockeys. People could watch horse races on television while they ate. Johnny liked to go to the restaurants to eat, because fans respected his privacy there. He also spent more time with Reuven Katz, his friend and business manager, and Reuven's wife, Catie.

Johnny moved into a house overlooking the Ohio River in Cincinnati.

He was busy. He got married again, this time to a woman named Laura. They had a son named Robert. A few years later, they were divorced.

In 1989, six years after his retirement and during the first year he was eligible, Johnny was elected to the Baseball Hall of Fame. It was a great honor. Al Barlick, Red Schoendienst, and Carl Yastrzemski were also inducted.

When he was inducted, Laura was pregnant with Robert. "As you saw her stand up, you will notice that there are several scouts already interested," he joked during his speech.

Bob Hope invited Johnny on another USO tour. Johnny flew to the Persian Gulf in the early 1990s during Operation Desert Storm to visit troops. Back home, he also continued to be involved in the Johnny Bench Scholarship Fund, which he established in 1983 after he retired. It gave college scholarships to under-privileged kids from both Cincinnati, Ohio, and

Bench laughs as Pee Wee Reese leans over to congratulate him during Bench's 1989 induction into the Baseball Hall of Fame. Baseball great Carl Yastrzemski sits on Bench's right.

Binger, Oklahoma. Johnny did many things to raise money for the fund, even appearing as a sports celebrity on the television game show *Who Wants to Be a Millionaire?*

Johnny participated in more baseball-related activities. He hosted a radio show in Cincinnati with Marty Brennaman. He made instructional videos to help young players. He also wrote books, like *The Complete Idiot's*

Guide to Baseball (with co-author Larry Burke). He worked with the Reds in their minor league system helping catchers and batters.

Johnny spent more time playing golf, too. He had been playing in the off-season for many years. Though he was never as good at golf as he was at baseball, once he retired from baseball he began to improve. People said that he had the power to hit a golf ball a long distance, but he lacked the precision. In baseball, he needed to get the ball out of the park. In golf, he needed to get the ball into a very small hole. Johnny said that he didn't have enough time to devote to golf to become great at it. "It was instinct in baseball," Johnny said. "You reacted when you catch the ball. You reacted when you see the ball. There's way too much time to think [in golf]."

In 1996, he met Elizabeth Benton. She was also a golfer. They met at ex-president Gerald Ford's invitational golf tournament in Vail, Colorado, but didn't really notice each other. Johnny offered to lend his condominium

In Dayton, Ohio, Johnny Bench and his son Robby run with the Olympic Flame as it makes its way to Salt Lake City in time for the 2002 Winter Olympics. No matter where he goes, Johnny's heart has always remained close to his home town—Robby's middle name is Binger.

in Palm Springs to a friend of Elizabeth's for the U.S. Golf Association Mid-Amateur tournament. Johnny wasn't planning to use the house that weekend. But when Elizabeth's friend couldn't make it, Johnny decided to go after all. Elizabeth and Johnny started dating shortly after. They married in February 1997.

Bench places the home plate during a ceremony to mark the location of the Cincinnati Reds' new stadium, the Great American Ball Park, on October 4, 2000.

Johnny was a pretty good golfer. In 1997, when he turned fifty, he became eligible for the PGA Seniors Tour.

Johnny also spent as much time with Robby as he could. By the time Robby was seven, he was already four feet eight inches tall—much taller than Johnny had been at that age! Robby played Little League ball and golfed with his father. Johnny said he just wanted his son to get a great education.

Around that time, Johnny also began to give motivational speeches to companies. He gave a speech called "The Vowels of Success." He also began to take an even more active role with the Reds. Jim Bowden, the team's general manager, invited Johnny to help coach in Florida for spring training. He was given the title of Special Assistant. In October of 2000, Johnny was present for the groundbreaking of the Great American Ball Park, a field designed to replace Riverfront Stadium in Cincinnati. Johnny wore a Reds' cap and crouched down in his old position at home plate.

JOHNNY LEE BENCH
CINCINNATI, N.L., 1967-1983
REDEFINED STANDARDS BY WHICH CATCHERS ARE
MEASURED DURING 17 SEASONS WITH "BIG RED MACHINE".
CONTROLLED GAME ON BOTH SIDES OF PLATE WITH
HIS HITTING (389 HOMERS-RECORD 327 AS A CATCHER,
1,376 RBI'S), THROWING OUT OPPOSING BASE RUNNERS,
CALLING PITCHES AND BLOCKING HOME PLA
MVP, 1970 AND 1972. WON 10 GOLD GLOVES. I
9TH INNING HOMER LED TO 1972 PENNANT.

Bench is considered the greatest catcher who ever lived, and his Hall of Fame
plaque marks his place in history. Besides his contributions to the Reds as a player,
his innovative catching style is imitated everywhere baseball is played.

Afterward, newspaper columnist Tim Sullivan wrote an article titled "How About Manager Bench?" in the *Cincinnati Enquirer*. In it, he suggested that Johnny would make a good manager for the Cincinnati Reds. Some people said that Johnny wasn't right for the job because he had never managed before. They said that because he was a Hall of Famer, his standards would be too high.

"I think if you've got a good ballclub that knows what they're doing, there are probably about six or seven games in a season where your manager can make a difference," Johnny responded in the *Cincinnati Enquirer*. "The manager's job is to make people feel good about coming to the ballpark, excited to play and believing they have a chance of winning." He went on to say that "Sparky [Anderson] told me, 'You should never manage.' He said, 'Great players should never be booed, and you know you're going to get booed if you're a manager.'" Johnny has not yet become the manager of the Cincinnati Reds.

Johnny Bench's Stats, 1967–1983

YR.	AVG.	G	AB	R	H	2B	3B	HR	RBI	BB	K
1967	.163	26	86	7	14	3	1	1	6	5	19
1968	.275	154	564	67	155	40	2	15	82	31	96
1969	.293	148	532	83	156	23	1	26	90	49	86
1970	.293	158	605	97	177	35	4	45	148	54	102
1971	.238	149	562	80	134	19	2	27	61	49	83
1972	.270	147	538	87	145	22	2	40	125	100	84
1973	.253	152	557	83	141	17	3	25	104	83	83
1974	.280	160	621	108	174	38	2	33	129	80	90
1975	.283	142	530	83	150	39	1	28	110	65	108
1976	.234	135	465	62	109	24	1	16	74	81	95
1977	.275	142	494	67	136	34	2	31	109	58	95
1978	.260	120	393	52	102	17	1	23	73	50	83
1979	.276	130	464	73	128	19	0	22	80	67	73
1980	.250	114	360	52	90	12	0	24	68	41	64
1981	.309	52	178	14	55	8	0	8	25	17	21
1982	.258	119	399	44	103	16	0	13	38	36	58
1983	.255	110	310	32	79	15	2	12	54	24	38

Postseason Stats

YR.	AVG.	G	AB	R	H	2B	3B	HR	RBI	BB	K
1970	.214	8	28	5	6	0	0	2	4	4	3
1972	.293	12	41	7	12	2	1	2	3	6	8
1973	.263	5	19	1	5	2	0	1	1	2	3
1975	.167	10	42	6	7	2	0	1	4	3	10
1976	.444	7	27	7	12	2	1	3	7	1	3
1979	.250	3	12	1	3	0	1	1	1	2	2

Source: SportsIllustrated.com

Sparky was right: Johnny was a great ballplayer. In 1999, Johnny was voted an All-Century Catcher. He told the *Cincinnati Enquirer* that standing with his fellow All-Century players "was sort of like playing with the Reds. We were pretty good." He continues to appear on experts' lists of the greatest players of all time.

"I changed catching," he said at the All-Century induction ceremony. He was right, too. Every catcher who has played the game since Johnny retired has had a higher standard to live up to—all this from a boy who started by swinging at milk cans in Binger, Oklahoma.

JOHNNY BENCH *TIMELINE*

1947 Johnny Bench born in Oklahoma City, Oklahoma.

1965 Johnny drafted by Cincinnati Reds.

1968 Johnny wins Rookie of the Year Award.

1970 The Reds win the National League pennant, but lose the World Series to the Baltimore Orioles.

1972 The Reds win the National League pennant, but lose the World Series to the Oakland A's.

1973 The Reds win the western division pennant, but lose to the New York Mets in the playoffs.

1975 The Reds beat the Boston Red Sox to win the World Series.

⚾	**1975**	Johnny has major shoulder surgery.
⚾	**1976**	The Reds beat the New York Yankees to win the World Series.
⚾	**1979**	The Reds win the eastern division pennant, but lose to the Los Angeles Dodgers in the playoffs.
⚾	**1979**	Johnny publishes *Catch You Later*, his autobiography, co-written with William Brashler.
⚾	**1983**	Johnny retires.
⚾	**1989**	Johnny elected to Hall of Fame on first ballot.
⚾	**1999**	Johnny voted All-Century catcher.

Glossary

all-star A player voted to be the best at his position.

AstroTurf Artificial grass used in many sports stadiums.

battery A term referring to the two-person grouping of the pitcher and the catcher.

batting average The number of a player's hits divided by the number of his at-bats. Used to calculate how often a player gets hits.

Big Red Machine A term used to describe the Cincinnati Reds during the 1970s, when they won several pennant races and the World Series.

cleanup slot The fourth position in the batting order.

Gold Glove Award   An award given to the best fielder at each position.

leadoff slot   The first position in the batting order.

minor leagues   The system of teams that Major League clubs use to train players for the team.

Riverfront Stadium   The stadium in Cincinnati where the Cincinnati Reds played between the early 1970s and the late 1990s.

runs batted in (RBI)   A number measuring how many times a batter has helped runners to score.

the show   A term used by baseball players to describe Major League Baseball.

triple A (AAA)   The highest level of team in the minor leagues.

For More Information

Organizations

The Cincinnati Reds
100 Main Street
Cincinnati, OH 45202
(513) 421-4510
Web site: http://reds.mlb.com

Field Of Dreams Baseball Tours
P.O. Box 270101
Oklahoma City, OK 73137-0101
(405) 682-6160
Web site: http://www.baseballtrips.com/

The Johnny Bench Scholarship Fund
200 West Fourth Street
Cincinnati, OH 45202
Web site: http://www.johnnybench.com/
scholarship_fund.php

National Baseball Hall of Fame and Museum
25 Main Street
P.O. Box 590
Cooperstown, NY 13326
(888) 425-5633
Web site: http://www.baseballhalloffame.org

The Office of the Commissioner of Baseball
245 Park Avenue, 31st floor
New York, NY 10167
(212) 931-7800
Web site: http://www.mlb.com

Society For American Baseball Research
812 Huron Road
Suite 719
Cleveland, OH 44115
(212) 575-0500
Web site: http://www.sabr.org

Films

Baseball: A Film by Ken Burns, 1994.
Field of Dreams by Phil Alden Robinson, 1989.

Web Sites

Due to the changing nature of Internet links, the Rosen Publishing Group, Inc., has developed an online list of Web sites related to the subject of this book. This site is updated regularly. Please use this link to access the list:

http://www.rosenlinks.com/bhf/jben/

For Further Reading

Anderson, Sparky, and Si Burick. *The Main Spark: Sparky Anderson and the Cincinnati Reds*. New York: Doubleday, 1978.

Anderson, Sparky and Dan Ewald. *They Call Me Sparky*. Chelsea, MI: Sleeping Bear Press, 1998.

Bench, Johnny, and William Brashler. *Catch You Later*. New York: Harper & Row, 1979.

Bench, Johnny, and Larry Burke. *The Complete Idiot's Guide to Baseball*. Indianapolis, IN: Alpha Books, 1999.

Bench, Johnny, Rich Piling, and Paul Cunningham. *Major League Baseball's Best Shots*. New York: DK Publishing, 2000.

James, Bill and Don Zminda and Neil Munro. *Stats All-Time Major League Handbook*. New York: Ballantine Books, 2000.

Kasoff, Jerry. *Baseball Just For Kids: Skills, Strategies and Stories To Make You A Better Ballplayer*. Englewood Cliffs, NJ: Grand Slam Press, Inc., 1996.

Morgan, Joe and Richard Lally. *Baseball For Dummies*. Foster City, CA: IDG Books Worldwide, 2000.

National Geographic, editors. *Baseball as America: Seeing Ourselves Through Our National Game*. Washington, DC: National Geographic Society, 2002.

Rhodes, Greg and John Erardi. *Big Red Dynasty: How Bob Hawsam and Spark Anderson Built the Big Red Machine*. Cincinnati, OH: Road West Publishing, 1997.

Rhodes, Greg, and John Snyder. *Redleg Journal: Year by Year and Day by Day with the Cincinnati Reds Since 1866*. Cincinnati, OH: Road West Publishing Company, 2000.

The Sporting News, editors. *Baseball's Greatest Players*. St. Louis, MO: Sporting News Publishing, 1998.

Bibliography

Baseball Almanac, "Johnny Bench."
    Retrieved April 26, 2002
    (http://www.baseball-almanac.com).

Bench, Johnny, and William Brashler.
    Catch You Later. New York: Harper &
    Row, 1979.

Cincinnati Post, "Johnny Bench Raises
    $250K." September 19, 2001. Retrieved
    April 28, 2002 (http://www.cincypost.com/
    2001/sep/19/bench091901.html).

Cincinnati Reds, "Cincinnati Reds Historical
    Stats." Retrieved April 6, 2002
    (http://cincinnati.reds.mlb.com).

Furman, Andy. *Cincinnati Post*. "Bench says
    he wanted to help Brennaman." July 28,
    2000. Retrieved April 20, 2002
    (http://www.cincypost.com/sports/2000/
    furman072800.html).

Graham, Janet. *Cincinnati Post*. "Bench Preparing For Run at Senior Tour." May 20, 1997. Retrieved April 20, 2002 (http://www.cincypost.com/sports/1997/bench052097.html).

Haft, Chris. *Cincinnati Enquirer*. "Bench: 'I Changed Catching'." October 25, 1999. Retrieved April 20, 2002 (http://reds.enquirer.com/1999/10/25/red_bench_i_changed.html).

James, Bill. *The Bill James Historical Baseball Abstract*. New York: Villard Books, 1988.

Lahman, Sean. "Pete Rose FAQ." April 10, 2002. Retrieved April 20, 2002 (http://www.baseball1.com/bb-data/rose/rose-faq.html).

Major League Baseball. "Hall of Fame Inductees." Retrieved April 5, 2002 (http://www.mlb.com).

National Baseball Hall of Fame. "Johnny Bench." Retrieved April 5, 2002 (http://www.baseballhalloffame.org).

RobertoClemente21.com. "Biography." Retrieved April 20, 2002 (http://www.robertoclemente21.com).

SportsIllustrated.com. "Johnny Bench." Retrieved April 6, 2002 (http://sportsillustrated.cnn.com).

Sullivan, Tim. *Cincinnati Enquirer*. "Bench Can't Catch A Break." September 19, 1998. Retrieved April 27, 2002 (http://enquirer.com/columns/sullivan/1998/09/091998ts.html).

Sullivan, Tim. *Cincinnati Enquirer*. "Bench pondering return to uniform—as manager." October 25, 1999. Retrieved October 23, 2002 (http://reds.enquirer.com/1999/10/25/red_bench_pondering.html).

Sullivan, Tim. *Cincinnati Enquirer*, "How About Manager Bench?" October 5, 2000. Retrieved April 20, 2002 (http://reds.enquirer.com/2000/10/05/red_sullivan_how_about.html).

Index

About the Author

Jesse Jarnow is a writer and editor based in Brooklyn, New York. He writes mostly about loud music and big explosions. His work has appeared in *Signal to Noise*, *Relix* magazine, *11211*, *Hear/Say*, and the *Anonymous Church of the Hypocritical Prophet*. He is a graduate of the Oberlin College creative writing department and a former member of the Studio 77 Art Collective.

Photo Credits

Cover, pp. 4, 8, 15, 28, 34, 54–55 64, 68 © Bettmann/Corbis; p. 6 © The Topps Company; p. 11 © DavidBurkett/www.hallowedground.org; pp. 12, 16, 19, 31, 33, 37, 39, 42, 50, 63, 67, 70, 73, 76–77, 78, 80, 84, 87, 89, 90, 92 © AP/Wide World Photos.

Editor

Jill Jarnow

Series Design and Layout

Geri Giordano